TEN DAYS

Ten Days in a New Life
Short Lessons for Newcomers

Ten Days – Ten Short Lessons for Newcomers

By: Carlton L. Coon, Sr.

Copyright – 2019 by Carlton L. Coon Sr.

All rights reserved. Written permission must be secured from the author and publisher to use or reproduce any part of this book, except for brief quotations in critical reviews or articles.

Unless otherwise noted quotations are from the King James Version of the Bible.

Information on other material: CarltonCoonSr.com

Editing: Pam Eddings

ISBN-13: 9781090332622

Printed in the United States of America

Contents

Letter from Pastor 3

Ten Days: Help in Orienting to a New Life 7

Using Your *Ten Days* Book 7

Day One: It Happened! 9

Day Two: Live Sure 15

Day Three: Be Prayerful 19

Day Four: Live in God's Word - the Bible 23

Day Five: Faithful is a Good Thing 27

Day Six: Submission is Not a Bad Word 31

Day Seven: Learn – Be a Disciple 33

Day Eight: Be a Thinker 37

Day Nine: Get Together 39

Day Ten: Grace and Graciousness 41

Congratulations! 43

Ten Days:
Help in Orienting to a New Life

Beginnings matter! The trajectory of a rocket launch affects the success of a mission. Vast energy is expended getting the rocket beyond the pull of earth's gravity.

You have "blasted off" into a new season of life. The Bible even calls it being "a new creature," (2 Corinthians 5:17). ***Ten Days*** is designed to help launch your Christian life at the right trajectory.

Use this tool as intended, and there will be great long-term benefit to your life.

Using Your *Ten Days* Book

Things you need:
1. A Bible for reading and for filling in the blanks. The particular book you are using is based on the King James Version of the Bible. If you do not have a King James Version, there is easy access online. (www.biblegateway.com
2. A pen or pencil for notes and answers.
3. You may also want to have a separate journal or note pad to write down questions or ideas that come to mind as you use ***Ten Days.***

Directions:
1. Read each scripture carefully. Based on what you read, fill in each blank with the right words.
2. Spend some time thinking about each of the scriptures you read. The time you spend thinking is a preliminary step to meditating on the Word of God. This type of meditating is not mystical. Instead, it is a healthy mental review of what you have read and studied.
3. Answer each question in the review area for each day.

You are ready to launch. Please pray a simple prayer. Ask the Lord to open your understanding of the Bible. Ask Jesus to increase your knowledge of Him, His way, and His will for your life.

Day One:
It Happened!

Salvation is a word used to describe a sinner having been saved from the result of sin. Salvation also indicates having been saved from continuing in the old life of sin. Salvation is needed by all. None of us are good on our own merit.

To experience salvation is not something based on our emotions. To *know* we are saved is not dependent on our emotions. Of course, a positive feeling will likely be a benefit that comes with having been "born again." But, salvation is not based on experience or emotion.

Instead, salvation depends on having <u>faith</u> in the saving <u>grace</u> of the Lord Jesus Christ and on the promises found in the Bible. Perhaps the words faith and grace are not clearly defined in your mind.

Faith is a complete trust or confidence. A good word picture of faith is an elevator.

> When we get on, we press the button for our desired floor. There is no question in our mind as to whether the elevator will take us to the destination. We have confidence in the outcome. Saving faith is similar. We trust God and His Word. We have confidence for the outcome.

Biblical *grace* is the unmerited favor of Jesus Christ toward us. Every person who is ever saved, will have been saved because of undeserved favor.

Circumstances may cause your feelings to go from high to low. Faith, that confidence in God, is what keeps you steady regardless of how you feel.

    A. This confidence is based on <u>the Bible, God's Word</u>.

God's desire is that all men would be saved and have eternal life.

John 3:16 contains a promise and an explanation. Through Christ Jesus we are able to have everlasting life. Everlasting life is not simply the length of life; it is also a quality of life. None of us can be good enough or do enough good works to gain everlasting life.

Our salvation comes only by the grace and mercy of God.

"For God so loved the _____ that he gave his only begotten _____, that whosoever believeth in him _____ _____ perish, but have everlasting life," (John 3:16).

"But God commendeth His _____ toward us, in that, while we were yet _____, Christ _____ for us" (Romans 5:8)

"For by _____ are ye saved through _____; and that not of yourselves: it is the _____ of God: Not of _____, lest any man should boast," (Ephesians 2:8-9).

    B. Your confidence is based on faith that led you to be obedient to God's design of salvation as it is given in the Bible.

Acts chapter 2 begins the era of salvation that came as a result of the death, burial, and resurrection of Jesus Christ. Acts 2 reports the birth of the New Testament Church. This beginning of the Church happened on the ancient Jewish feast known as "The Feast of Pentecost."

At the "Feast of Pentecost," an early church leader by the name of Simon Peter explained the message of salvation. Peter's message came after a multitude of people had seen the first outpouring of the Holy Spirit on this new era of believers. These onlookers had several questions about what was happening.

(Slowly read Acts chapter two. Make notes of things you find interesting or questions that come to mind.)

The final thrust of Peter's speech that day was in regard to the death, burial, and resurrection of Jesus Christ. Some of these onlookers had participated in the conspiracy that resulted in Jesus' death. Peter charged his listeners, making them responsible for the crucifixion of the Lord Jesus Christ, (Acts 2:36). What a terrible crime! These people had been part of the murder of a good man who had never harmed anyone. Their response to Peter's indictment of their sin:

Now when they _____ this, they were pricked in their _____, and said unto Peter and to the rest of the apostles, Men and brethren, what shall we do?" _____

The mass of people were asking if there was a remedy for their being conspirators to the death of their Messiah. I doubt anything in your past life would match having participated in the death of the Lord Jesus Christ.

Simon Peter's response gave them a process to obey.

Then Peter said unto them, _____, and be _____ every one of you in the name of _____ _____ for the _____ of sins, and ye shall receive the gift of the _____ _____. For the _____ is unto you, and to your _____, and to _____ that are afar off, even as many as the Lord our God shall call," (Acts 2:37-39).

    C. Your sin may be nothing like what this group had been involved in. Obeying Peter's instruction brought an assurance of salvation to these conspirators to murder. Be sure in your mind, whether you feel sure or not. Your sin has certainly been addressed as you have obeyed Simon Peter's instructions. <u>You repented of your sins, have been baptized in the name of Jesus Christ, and received the gift of the Holy Ghost</u>.

What have you done? Well, you repented!

Repentance involves not only asking for forgiveness, but also doing an "about face" regarding sinful behavior. Repentance means you will no longer participate in the sins you once did.

"Repent ye therefore, and be _____, that your sins may be _____ out, when the times of refreshing shall come from the presence of the Lord," (Acts 3:19).

   D. Your assurance is also based on having been buried with Christ by baptism in His name.

When we are baptized in the name of Jesus Christ, as instructed in Acts 2, our sins are remitted. The word "remit" means to "remove this item."

Therefore we are _____ with him by baptism into death: that like as Christ was raised up from the _____ by the glory of the Father, even so we also should _____ in newness of life, (Romans 6:4).

The like figure whereunto even _____ doth also now save us (not the putting away of the filth of the flesh, but the answer of a good conscience toward God,) by the resurrection of Jesus Christ, (I Peter 3:21).

   E. Your certainty comes from having received the Holy Ghost. You know you received the Holy Ghost, because you experienced <u>the initial sign of speaking in tongues</u>. This happened on the day of Pentecost (and later) <u>when people were filled with the Holy Spirit</u>. (Acts 2:4)

While Peter yet spake these words, the _____ _____ fell on all of them which heard the word. And they of the circumcision which believed were astonished, as many as came with Peter, because that on the _____ also was poured out the _____ of the Holy Ghost. For they _____ them speak with _____, and magnify God, (Acts 10:44-46).

12

And when Paul had laid his hands upon them, the _____ _____ came on them: and they spake with _____, and prophesied, (Acts 19:6).

Review

- Jesus died, was buried in a tomb, and rose again physically. We do the same in a spiritual way by doing what three things?
    1. _____
    2. _____
    3. _____

- On occasion we may not feel as though we are saved due to emotions. What gets us through these times?-
    _____
    _____
    _____
    _____

- God's grace has provided you the possibility of being saved. What then leads to obedience? _____
    _____

- When a person receives the infilling of the Holy Ghost according to the Scripture, what supernatural sign will be experienced?_____
    _____
    _____
    _____

Day Two:
Live Sure

Most people enjoy telling a story about meaningful things that happen to them. You may not fully realize it now, but your salvation is the greatest thing in your life. Salvation, also spoken of as a *new birth*, impacts both time and eternity.

You probably want others to have the same experience. You may have several friends and family members who have terrible habits. Addiction, an out of control desire for wealth, or pornography controls so many people. Those people need to hear <u>your story</u> of salvation.

    A. We are told to share the story of our experience.

You are saved because someone shared the Gospel with you. It may have been a preacher in a pulpit, or a friend. You heard what they had to say, and you have benefitted. It is now both your privilege and duty to influence others to consider Jesus. People in your circle of influence need hope.

They need the life change that only the Lord Jesus Christ can bring. Better than your pastor or anyone, your story can point your friends and family toward that change. They know you and will be impacted by what you have to say. Jesus was clear on what He wanted His followers to do.

And Jesus came and spake unto them, saying: All _____ is given unto me in _____ and in _____. Go ye therefore, and teach all nations, baptizing them in the name of the _____ _____, and Holy Ghost (Matthew 28:18-19).

But when the _____ is come, whom I will send unto you from the Father…, he shall _____ of me, (John 15:26).

    B. We are given the power we need to witness to others.

Sometimes we struggle to tell someone else our story. Some of us are shy or timid; others may not feel knowledgeable enough about the Bible. Neither of those is a good reason. The Holy Ghost gives us power to tell our story. It's simple: just tell your experience. In court proceedings, a witness can only tell about things experienced. The same is true here. Tell your story. Jesus will give you boldness and the necessary knowledge to be effective. Read Jesus' promise about telling your story.

But ye shall receive power, after that the _____ _____ is come upon you: and ye shall be witnesses unto me both in Jerusalem, and in all Judea, and in Samaria, and unto the _____ part of the earth, (Acts 1:8).

   C. Write your story on this page. Tell about your past life, how you heard the Gospel and what Jesus has done in your life. Writing your story is important. Writing helps clarify what you will say to others as you tell your story.

_____
_____
_____
_____
_____
_____
_____
_____
_____
_____

Review

- According to Scripture, what message should you share with others? _____

- What empowers us to share the Gospel message with others? _____

- List at least three people you will share your experience with this week.

    1. _____
    2. _____
    3. _____

Day Three:
Be Prayerful

With your salvation, also called a *new birth*, you became a child of God. God is your Father. A good relationship between a father and child is built on communication. The way to really know someone is through regular communication.

Prayer is simple. Prayer is "talking (communicating) with the Lord Jesus Christ." Prayer does not have to be loud or boisterous, though it can be. Communicating with God is an important part of your new life. *Ten Days* introduces you to prayer. What is provided is only a beginning. There is much to learn about prayer. Your pastor will have recommendations for you to read, watch or listen to.

Ten Days can help establish a time of daily devotion. Initially, your daily time in prayer may be brief. Don't worry. Getting started is half of the battle. Launching a life of prayer is important for several reasons.

    A. Prayer builds your relationship with the Lord Jesus Christ.

In prayer, you speak with the Lord Jesus Christ. But, it is not a one-way conversation. There will be times, when you will know God has spoken something to your mind. In most cases, what you feel is only for your help and is not to be lightly shared with others. In such moments, you come to know God more intimately.

Prayer also unleashes God's power. He is then able to work on your behalf. Prayer is what allows God to bring blessing to your life. Prayer is also the place where you speak to the Lord on behalf of others. Prayer opens doors of opportunity for God to work. Prayer <u>must</u> be part of your life for you to build a relationship with the Lord Jesus.

Rejoicing in _____: patient in tribulation: _____ instant in prayer, (Romans 12:12).

For it is _____ by the word of _____ and prayer, (I Timothy 4:5).

    B. Jesus prayed as our example.

Jesus prayed often. If Jesus Christ, being God in flesh, prayed, how much more do we need to pray? Jesus' disciples asked Him to teach them to pray. In response, Jesus gave instruction on the subject of prayer.

After this manner therefore pray ye: (9) Our _____ which art in heaven, Hallowed be _____ name: (10) Thy Kingdom come. Thy will be done in earth, as it is in heaven.(11) Give us this day our daily bread.(12) And forgive us our debts, as we forgive our debtors.(13) And lead us not into temptation, but deliver us from evil: For thine is the kingdom, and the power, and the glory forever. Amen, (Matthew 6:9-13).

And in the _____, rising up a great while before day, he went out, and departed into a _____ place, and there _____, (Mark 1:35).

    C. Jesus' followers saw the need for prayer.

And it came to pass, that, as he was _____ in a certain place, when he ceased, one of his disciples and unto him, Lord, teach us to pray, as John also taught his disciples, (Luke 11:1).

But we will give ourselves _____ to prayer, and to the _____ of the word, (Acts 6:4).

Review

- List below three things that prayer will do.

    1. _____

2. _____

3. _____

- It is very important for you to pray at least once a day. Place a time when you will schedule prayer on each day of the coming week.

Mon. _____

Tues. _____

Wed. _____

Thurs._____

Fri. _____

Sat. _____

Sun. _____

Day Four:
Live in God's Word - the Bible

The Bible is a vital link between you and God. The Bible is God's Word for us. (If you have not yet had a Personal Bible Study, ask someone at your church how to schedule such a study.) The Bible contains authority and wisdom for daily living. Through the Bible, God will guide and strengthen you. The Bible is a handbook for survival.

You should read a portion of the Bible each day. Read for understanding, rather than to say you have read the Bible. Beyond reading, contemplate what you have read throughout the day.

    A. The Bible is the inspired Word of God.

The Bible is the inspired word of God given for our instruction. The word "inspiration" used in the next verse means: *God breathed*. The Bible is not a collection put together by men, though God used men. The Bible you read from is a "God book."

It gives us the history and future of all God's creation. The Bible tells of man's downfall, but also points to God's grace.

All scripture is given by _____ of God, and is profitable for _____, for reproof, for _____, for _____ in righteousness, (II Timothy 3:16).

So then _____ cometh by _____, and hearing by the _____ of God, (Romans 10:17).

    B. God's Word is the source of Life.

Your human body needs food. So does the spiritual part of your life. The Bible contains needed spiritual food. Growth comes by reading, studying, and contemplating the Bible each day.

But he answered and said, It is _____, Man shall not _____ by bread alone, but by every _____ that proceedeth out of the mouth of God, (Matthew 4:4.).

C. God's Word is a source of contentment.

Peace comes when we live consistent with the Word of God. Studying the Bible is where we learn His principles. By learning and applying these principles, we align ourselves with Him. His way is the most effective way to life.

But he said, Yea rather, _____ are they that hear the _____ of God, and keep it, (Luke 11:28).

D. God's Word gives direction.

Always look to God and His Word for direction in life.

Thy word is a _____ unto my feet, and a _____ unto my path, (Psalm 119:105).

E. God's Word is a Weapon.

On one occasion, Jesus fasted forty days. When the fast ended, Satan came to tempt Jesus. Jesus responded to each temptation with a verse from the Old Testament. It was Jesus' weapon to overcome temptation and the devil.

Scriptures will also work as a weapon for you. At times you will come under attack. The attack may come through depression, finances, fear, loneliness, guilt, shame, fear, or various forms of temptation. Where the devil attacks, find scriptures relating to that situation and begin quoting the verses, and thinking about them until you have gained victory.

And when the tempter came to him, he said, If _____ be the Son of God, command that these stones be made bread. But he answered and said, It is _____, Man shall not live by _____ alone, but by every _____ that proceedeth out of the mouth of God, (Matthew 4:3-4).

For the _____ of God is quick, and powerful, and _____ than any two-edged sword, piercing even to the dividing asunder of soul and spirit, and of the _____ and morrow, and is a _____ of the thoughts and intents of the heart, (Hebrews 4:12).

Recommended approach to gaining benefit from your Bible. Read a single paragraph in Acts 2. Think about what it says. Make notes as to what happened as the church was being started.

Review

- List three things the Bible is to be for us.

1. _____

2. _____

3. _____

- List one or more ways Satan has attacked you. Then find scriptures concerning that attack; write them down. Put them on index cards to carry along with you to memorize. These verses will help you gain victory in the area of your life.

_____

_____

_____

_____

_____

- Will you continue reading a paragraph from Acts each day? Make notes and learn all you can about what is being said.

Day Five:
<u>Faithful</u> is a Good Thing

Consistency is a rare pearl. No person becomes a mature Christian by an occasional encounter with God. Develop consistency in prayer, working to gain benefit from your Bible and in church attendance.

Faithful church attendance is important. Every service is different. Some services will build you up; others will equip you to serve, while others extend an invitation to the unsaved. At any of these gatherings, you will experience elements needed to improve your relationship with the Lord Jesus Christ.

King David said, "I was glad when they said unto me, Let us go into the house of the Lord," (Psalm 122:1). There are several reasons to be consistent with your church attendance.

    A. At church you will find good fellowship.

Fellowship is friendship and connecting to others in a practical way. Such connecting is a vital part of Christian life.

Christian life is never done in isolation. None of the people at your church are perfect. If you look closely, you will quickly find flaws. Of course, the same can be said of you. Connecting with your church's imperfect people who are also dealing with life's difficulties will strengthen and encourage you.

Those in the early church understood the value of fellowship. Another good word for the experience of *fellowship* is partnership. As a church we partner together.

And they _____ steadfastly in the _____ doctrine and _____, and in breaking of bread, and in prayers, (Acts 2:42).

That which we have _____ and heard _____ we unto you, that ye also may have _____ with us: and truly our

_____ is with the Father, and with his Son Jesus Christ, (I John 1:3).

    B. Church is the place where you will be encouraged.

At times you will be discouraged. While you are at church; a song, a kind word, or the preaching or teaching will encourage you.

And let us _____ one another to provoke unto _____ and to _____ works: Not forsaking the _____ of ourselves together, as the manner of some is; but exhorting one another; and so much the _____, as you see the day approaching, (Hebrews 10:24-25).

    C. Church is the place where you will receive much teaching and instruction.

You may know a great deal about the Bible and what it teaches. If so, you are somewhat rare. Knowledge about the Bible is often lacking. Yet, as you have already learned, the Bible is important to your Christian life.

Teaching is one of God's gifts to the church. As you are taught, your relationship with God will mature. You will begin to better understand why you should focus on certain behaviors. These please the Lord Jesus. You will also learn that mature Christians do not practice certain behaviors. At church we learn to address life's difficulties.

And He gave _____, apostles; and some, prophets; and some, evangelists; and some, _____ and teachers; For the _____ of the saints, for the work of the _____, for the edifying of the body of Christ, (Ephesian 4:11-12).

    D. At church, you can get involved in serving.

Through instruction, you will learn about the different gifts God has put into you. No person has exactly the same abilities and interests as another. Those unique gifts and abilities are needed by your church. You are not just to be saved – you are to serve God and others. It is through your church that you will have the opportunity to put your gifts to work.

Having then _____ differing according to the grace that is given to us, whether prophecy, let us _____ according to the proportion of faith; Or _____, let us wait on our ministering; or he that _____, on teaching; Or he that _____, on exhortation; he that giveth, let him do it with _____; he that ruleth, with diligence; he that _____ mercy, with cheerfulness, (Romans 12:6-8).

Review

- List four things you will gain by consistently attending church.

  1. _____
  2. _____
  3. _____
  4. _____

- List the five ministries God has provided for the church.

  1. _____
  2. _____
  3. _____
  4. _____
  5. _____

Day Six:
Submission is Not a Bad Word

God's Word instructs us to be in submission to the authority placed in our lives. The word *submission* is not one to fear. It was a military word meaning we are "to take our place in the rank." A marching army must all be unity, moving in the same direction. God has put a divine order of authority in the Church. Apostle Paul wrote that Christ is the head of the Church, (Colossians 1:18).

A. Your pastor.

One blessing God has given you is a *pastor*. The word "pastor" means *shepherd*. The leader of your church, the pastor, serves in the same way a shepherd does for a flock of sheep. A shepherd leads, feeds, seeks, and works to bring health to those in his flock. Your pastor will do the same for you.

B. Your pastor will teach and instruct you.

Your pastor will provide teaching and training. Here you will began to better understand the Bible. If you have a question, be sure to ask your pastor.

How then shall they call on him in whom they have not believed? And how shall they _____ in him of whom they have not heard? And how shall they _____ without a preacher? (Romans 10:14).

And He gave some, apostles; and some, prophets; and some evangelists; and some _____ and teachers; For the _____ of the saints, for the work of the _____, for the edifying of the body of Christ, (Ephesians 4:11).

C. Your Pastor will give you counsel.

There will be times when you are confused and have questions about spiritual matters, or life in general. Your pastor can help you get through these times and find the answers you need.

Remember them which have the rule over you, who have spoken unto you the _____ of God; whose _____ follow, _____ the end of their conversation, (Hebrews 13:7).

Where no _____ is, the people fall: but in the multitude of _____ there is safety, (Proverbs 11:14).

Review

- What gift has God given the church for spiritual authority?
  _____

- Name two things that you can receive from your pastor.
  1. _____
  2. _____

32

Day Seven:
Learn – Be a Disciple

Now that you have been born again, you are on a path to be a disciple of Christ Jesus. Being "born again" is not the end of your experience with God; it is the beginning.

A disciple is "one who learns." As you apply the content of the previous chapters, you are on a path to being a disciple of the Lord Jesus Christ. Christian discipleship never stops because we never stop learning.

Ask your pastor if your church has discipleship or orientation classes? If so, take advantage of these.

A. What is discipleship?

A disciple is "one who learns." Christian discipleship takes learning a step further. Jesus' disciples not only learn, they also put into practice what they learn. Assume the role of a student and look to God and the Bible to teach you.

For this _____ we also, since the day we _____ it, do not cease to pray for you, and to desire that ye might be _____ with the _____ of his will in all wisdom and _____ understanding; That ye might walk worthy of the Lord unto all _____, being fruitful in every good work, and _____ in the knowledge of God, (Colossians 1:9-10).

B. The cost of discipleship.

Being a disciple of Jesus is not always easy. Applying what we learn about Him will require change. A disciple never tries to justify a sinful lifestyle, but seeks to change their life to fit for Jesus. Through such change, you will find your true Christian life.

Then said Jesus unto his disciples, If any man will come _____ me, let him _____ himself, and take up his _____, and _____ me. For whosoever will _____ his life shall _____ it; and whosoever will lose his _____ for my sake shall find it, (Matthew 16:24-25).

And I will _____ at liberty; for I _____ thy precepts, (Psalm 119:45).

C. The benefits of discipleship.

While there is a cost involved with discipleship, the rewards are many. Many blessings come from being a disciple of the Lord Jesus Christ. These blessings happen now as well as in eternity.

1. Fruit of the Spirit.

Fruit is a result of what is in a tree. The Bible talks about "the fruit of the Spirit." As you can imagine, the fruit of the Spirit comes from a Spirit-filled life. When you are full of His Spirit, these qualities will be exhibited in your life.

Love	Joy	Peace
Longsuffering	Gentleness	Goodness
Faith	Meekness	Temperance

"But the _____ of the Spirit is love, joy, peace, _____, gentleness, goodness, faith, Meekness, _____; against such there is no law," (Galatians 5:22-23).

2. Financial blessings.

Some teach that serving Jesus assures one of wealth and prosperity. This is not correct. But, part of being a disciple of Christ is trusting Him regarding your finances. Jesus said that if we would be faithful over the few things He has blessed us with, He will make us ruler over many things. (Read Matthew 25:14-29.)

You have the opportunity to join others in your church in bringing tithe and offering. Not only does generous giving bless the Lord's work, but God also blesses those who give. Talk with your pastor and learn more about the blessing of giving.

Bring ye all the tithes into the storehouse, that there may be meat in mine house, and _____ me now herewith, saith the Lord of hosts, if I will not _____ you the windows of _____, and pour you out a _____, that there shall not be room enough to receive it, (Malachi 3:10).

Honor the Lord with thy _____, and with the _____ of all thine increase: so shall thy _____ be filled with plenty, and thy _____ shall burst out with new wine, (Proverbs 3:9-10).

Review

- What does it mean to be a disciple of Christ? _____
  _____

- What will our life exhibit as a result of being Spirit-filled?
  _____

- List two opportunities that God has provided for us to give back a portion of what He has blessed us with.

    1. _____
    2. _____

Day Eight:
Be a Thinker

"Think about what you are thinking about," is not a new concept. Your mind is powerful. The imagination can roam far afield if you don't pay attention to what you are thinking about. Your mind can move you toward old habits and old ways of thinking. Those who give attention to their thoughts take the first step toward controlling their mind.

Pay close attention to your thought life. Pay attention when your mind says, "You are too busy to pray," or "You are too tired to go to church." Letting those thoughts direct your action will result in a weak spiritual life or in being totally backslidden.

   A. You can't control each thought, but you can capture the bad thoughts.

At times we let temptation have a one-way conversation in our mind. If we do this, it would be like Jesus not having spoken back against Satan's temptations. When your thoughts are going the wrong direction, in your mind, speak against those wrong thoughts.

Casting down _____, and every high thing that exalteth itself against the knowledge of God, and bringing into _____ every _____ to the obedience of Christ; (2 Corinthians 10:5).

An ancient said, "You cannot keep a bird from flying overhead, but you can keep a bird from building a nest in your hair." This is true of your thoughts. A passing thought will often happen, but don't let that thought linger.

   B. Use the Bible's Thought Filter

The Bible gives an excellent filter as to how we should think. Apply this filter, and pornography, gossip, filthy language, violence, etc. will never control you.

Finally, brethren, whatsoever things are _____, whatsoever things *are* _____, whatsoever things *are* just, whatsoever things *are* _____, whatsoever things *are* _____, whatsoever things *are* of _____ _____; if *there be* any virtue, and if *there be* any _____, think on these things, (Philippians 4:8).

Review

- Honestly assess your own thought life. What are the un-Christian thoughts that are most likely to come through your mind?

  _____
  _____
  _____
  _____
  _____
  _____

- Look back at Philippians 4:8. Based on what it says to think about, should you watch an "R" rated movie that contains much sex, violence and vulgar language?

  _____
  _____

- Why not?

  _____
  _____
  _____
  _____

Day Nine:
Get Together

Christianity is intended to be a "together" experience. In part, this was addressed in an earlier session. But our being together is with the intent of being a benefit to others.

The New Testament uses the phrase, "one another" 47 times. Over sixty percent of those phrases come from the writings of Paul. Paul gives a significant amount of the instruction regarding Christian living in the New Testament. An example of the "one another" passages include the following:

> We are taught to be focused on "one another."
>
> "Bear one another's burdens."
>
> "Accept one another."

Not only will you need people, but others will also need you. The mutual effort to serve each other is one of the great characteristics of the church. We need "one another."

- Tolerate one another: Ephesians 4:2 With all _____ and meekness, with longsuffering, _____ one another in love…

- Forgive one another: Colossians 3:13 Forbearing one another, and _____ one another, if any man have a _____ against any: even as Christ forgave you, so also do ye.

- Seek good for one another: 1 Thessalonians 5:15 See that none render _____ for _____ unto any man; but ever follow that which is _____, both among yourselves, and to all men.

Review

Some people are introverted. Others are an extrovert. We serve "one another" in different ways. Don't feel as though you must serve others like anyone else does.

- In what way(s) do you see yourself being of help to someone else? (This can be practical or spiritual.)

  _____
  _____
  _____
  _____
  _____

- As you think about your own needs, challenges and weaknesses; how might you need someone else to help you?

  _____
  _____
  _____
  _____
  _____

Day Ten:
Grace and Graciousness

We are recipients of grace. Grace is the "unmerited favor of God." *Grace* is a gift given with no expectation of a return. Christians are to extend grace, or unmerited favor, toward other Christians and to those not yet saved.

The world around us has become vicious. Meanness and hurtful things are published on social media each day. Many of these are things we would never say to each other face-to-face. Jesus expects His followers to be different. We are to control our emotions and not let them drive our behavior.

In the thought of Biblical times, the word "heart" was used to describe a person's emotions. The heart was to be carefully guarded.

- Live graciously, wearing the "breastplate of right-living."

Don't let your emotions determine your responses. Ephesians introduces the armor of God. One component is the breastplate of righteousness.

Ephesians 6:13-14 Wherefore take unto you the whole _____ of God, that ye may be able to withstand in the evil day, and having done all, to stand. [14]Stand therefore, having your loins girt about with truth, and having on the breastplate of _____.

The word righteousness refers to "living right" or behaving in a just way. Living right must not depend on your emotions. Do right whether or not you feel like doing right.

You have received grace. Can you not now be gracious to others? Some do not deserve a kind word – speak a kind word anyway. Others have not been there when you needed them. As a Christian, would you now take the initiative to be there for them?

Christians who have received grace are to express grace to others.

Review

- What will you have to control to act in the right way?
  _____

- Which of life's challenges tend to cause you the greatest distress?
  _____
  _____
  _____
  _____

- How can you prepare yourself to deal with those challenges?
  _____
  _____
  _____
  _____

Congratulations!

You have made it through *Ten Days*. Continue to use the habits mentioned in this booklet to better establish you as a Christian. Please, participate in any classes or programs your church may offer to newcomers. With each new day you live for Jesus, you will see your life changed for the better. Your spirit will begin to soar to new heights with Him.

And remember each day to:

Live Sure

    Be Faithful – because Faithful is a Good Thing

        Be Prayerful

            Live in God's Word - the Bible

    Live to Share Your Story

    Live Gracefully

Live a Life of Learning

    Choose to Submit

        Think About What You are Thinking About

For information on other Christian Living material visit CarltonCoonsr.com.

Made in the USA
Columbia, SC
14 February 2025